Avoiding Foreign Intelligence Traps:

At Home and While Traveling Abroad

Most of the information in this book comes from publications of the Overseas Security Advisory Council. OSAC is a joint venture between State Department and private sector security professionals designed to exchange security-related information pertaining to foreign travel. OSAC may be contacted at (202) 663-0533. Information is available via the OSAC web site at http://www.ds-osac.org.

Some of the information comes from Mossad training materials.

It's your first visit to London and the head of your company's R&D program in San Jose sent you to brief one of your largest customers, the British office of Airbus on your latest software breakthrough in artificial intelligence. He could not make it, so you are selected because you did most of the software development. Anyway, you rented a car at Heathrow airport and checked into the hotel. So far, so good. That night you called California from the hotel room and received final instruction on what to say at the meeting to be held the next day. Although you want to impress the customer, you ask, "Should I mention we were able to _____ the ____ by _____ ? The head of R&D says, "Certainly not, that's proprietary information." He says, "If they ask, just say we are working on that and may be able to solve it. Ask if they have any specific requirements, they would like us to address in the product. We may be able to incorporate specific features they would like to see in a future software update."

The next day, the meetings in the customer's high security facility went well, and afterwards you head back to the hotel for dinner and a drink. On the way to the hotel you stop your car at a stoplight and the car behind you runs into your rental car. You are not hurt. Just ticked off that this would happen to you on your first trip to London. The guy in the car behind you comes to the window and apologizes profusely and readily admits it was his fault. He accepts full responsibility and asks if you are injured. It was such a small tap that you are surprised he even asked. You say you are unhurt and mention it is a rental car.

The driver notices your accent and asks if you are an American? You say "Yes.", and he says, "California? I have a cousin in Bakersfield." By now you get out of the car and only see a busted taillight. The driver tells you this is his first visit to England from Australia and he just can't get used to driving on the left.

The driver says you can avoid any difficulty with the rental company if he pays for the repair and he pulls out a wad of hundred-dollar bills from his coat pocket. He says that $5,000 ought to be enough for the repair, and holds out a stack of bills for you to take.

At first you hesitate, then think it would be so much easier to just pay the rental company in cash and avoid saying anything about the accident back at the company. It's obvious to you that such a minor amount of damage will cost less than $5,000 and take the money. That was your <u>second</u> mistake.

First of all, you were being recorded and someone now has a video of you accepting what is obviously a large amount of money from what you learn later on, is a known intelligence agent from a former soviet country. Telling you he was from Australia was a mistake that should have tipped you off since they drive on the left in Australia, but you missed that little nugget.

What was your first mistake? Mentioning the proprietary information on the hotel phone about your company's breakthrough in artificial intelligence. The hotel telephone was bugged not only by a foreign intelligence service that laid the trap for you, but also by British Intelligence. It would have made no difference if you had used your cell phone for the call since the room was bugged as well.

Basically, you fell into their trap and you are screwed. You are being recruited!

Table of Contents

1. You are the Target

The threat of foreign intelligence interests' targeting American travelers is well founded. During fiscal years 1995 through 1999, the Department of Energy (DOE) counter-intelligence officials and records identified over 75 incidents of attempted espionage by foreign nationals against travelers from only four laboratories.

The risk of becoming a target for recruitment by a foreign intelligence agency increases greatly during foreign travel. As an American government official, scientist, or business traveler with access to useful information, you can become the target of a foreign intelligence or security service at any time in any country. As described in "*Who's Doing What to Whom*", the threat is certainly not limited to so-called "unfriendly" countries.

Foreign travel controls generally focus on travel to "sensitive" countries—those countries considered to be a risk to national security, like Russia and China. One government agency found that travelers to non-sensitive countries often confront similar types of incidents as travelers to "sensitive" countries because foreign intelligence entities can operate worldwide. In fact, they can operate some of these same traps in the U.S.A.

Never think, "They wouldn't dare risk something like that against me. They have too much at stake." Many countries do risk it, routinely, because the potential benefits are great and the risks are very low when an intelligence service is operating on its home turf. Even U.S. Government cabinet level officials and corporate CEOs have been assigned to bugged hotel rooms and had all their documents secretly photographed or their laptop computers accessed.

Conversely, never think you are too low-ranking to be of interest. Secretaries, file clerks and cleaning crew are targeted because they can often provide access to valuable information.

Foreign intelligence organizations' efforts to obtain information from travelers often begin by identifying potential sources of information from visa applications. Travelers deemed of interest are then assessed by learning as much as possible about them. If the travelers continue to be of interest, various intelligence-gathering methods, such as baggage searches or surveillance, are used.

Foreign government scrutiny of you while visiting another country may occur by design or chance for any of the following reasons:
- You have government, business, scientific, or technical information of potential value to a foreign government or a local industry.
- You have relatives or organizational affiliations or speak the local language fluently in the country you are visiting.
- You fit a terrorism, narcotic trafficking, criminal, or other profile.
- You buy or sell on the black-market.
- The local government discovers on your person or in your luggage literature that is banned or strictly controlled.
- You are associating with individuals the host government considers as political dissidents.

Here are some of the common methods that may be used. Most activities directed against you will be conducted in an unobtrusive manner that you are very unlikely to notice. Others are sometimes conducted in a rather crude manner that is observable. Brief summaries of cases in which American travelers have reported such observations are found in *"In the Line of Fire: American Travelers Abroad."*

2. Methods of Recruitment

Assessment - Friendly discussion with local contacts who assess whether you have information of value and seek to identify any personal attitudes, beliefs, problems or needs that could be exploitable.

Elicitation - A ploy whereby seemingly normal conversation is contrived to extract intelligence information of value. Advantages of this technique are that it:
- Puts someone at ease to share information.
- Is difficult to recognize as an intelligence technique.
- Is easily deniable.

Eavesdropping - Listening to other peoples' conversations to gather information. Frequently done in social environments where attendees feel comfortable and secure and, therefore, are more likely to talk about themselves or their work. Frequent venues include restaurants, bars, and public transportation.
- Eavesdropping can occur in a radius of six to eight seats on public transportation or 10-12 feet in other settings.

Technical Eavesdropping - Use of audio and visual devices, usually concealed.
- Relatively cost efficient and low risk.
- Concealed devices can be installed in public and private facilities -- such as hotel rooms, restaurants, offices, and automobiles.

"Bag Operations" - Surreptitious entry into someone's hotel room to steal, photograph, or photocopy documents; steal or copy magnetic media; or download from laptop computers.
- Often conducted or condoned by host government intelligence or security services or by operatives for local corporations.
- Frequently done with cooperation of hotel staff.
- Surveillance - Following you to determine your contacts and activities. Labor intensive if done correctly. Not usually done unless you are suspected of improper activity or a target of great interest.

Theft of Information - Stealing documents, briefcases, laptop computers or sensitive equipment.
- Laptop computers are especially vulnerable as they may contain a treasure trove of information.
- Theft of laptops from hotel rooms and while transiting airports is especially common.
- Foreign service has plausible denial, as the laptop may have been stolen for the value of the laptop rather than value of the information it contained. You may never know whether the information was compromised or not.

2

Intercepting Electronic Communications - Telephones, fax, telex, and computers can all be monitored electronically. You are particularly vulnerable while communicating to, from or within foreign countries, as most foreign telecommunications systems cooperate with their country's security service.

- Office, hotel, and portable telephones (including cellular) are key targets.

3. How to Protect Yourself

Common sense and basic counter-intelligence (CI) awareness can effectively protect you against foreign attempts to collect sensitive, proprietary, and other privileged information. A few tips are listed below.

- Arrange a pre-travel briefing from your security office.
- Maintain physical control of all sensitive documents or equipment at all times. Do not leave items that would be of value to a foreign intelligence service unattended in hotel rooms or stored in hotel safes.
- Limit sensitive discussions -- hotel rooms or other public places are rarely suitable to discuss sensitive information.
- Do not use computer or facsimile equipment at foreign hotels or business centers for sensitive matters.
- Do not divulge information to anyone not authorized to hear it.
- Ignore or deflect intrusive inquiries or conversation about business or personal matters.
- Keep unwanted material until it can be disposed of securely. Burn or shred paper and cut floppy disks in pieces and discard.
- Keep your laptop computer as carry-on baggage -- never check it with other luggage and, if possible, remove or control storage media.
- If you must leave your laptop anywhere, assume it will be examined and files copied. Carry necessary files on a DVD-ROM or flash drive – and don't let anyone see it.
- If secure communications equipment is accessible, use it to discuss business matters.
- Don't trust anyone!
- Report any Counter-Intelligence incident to the relevant U.S. Government agency and/or your local security office.

Avoiding and Recognizing Foreign Intelligence Interest

While traveling abroad, you are on the other country's home turf where the local security and intelligence services have many resources available. They can monitor and, to some extent, control the environment in which you live and work. You, in turn, may be at a disadvantage, because you are on unfamiliar territory.

Allied as well as hostile intelligence and security organizations use their home field advantage to look for potential sources who can be developed and exploited based on greed, manipulation of psychological or emotional weaknesses, conflicting loyalties, addiction, or coercion. The local services routinely monitor black market activities, dissident groups, prostitution, certain bars, gay hangouts, gambling establishments, and other areas where human weaknesses may be observable.

Many Americans possess personality traits that increase their vulnerability to the classic routines of espionage.

- **Sociability:** Americans characteristically want to be liked. In order to gain approval, we tend to be social and gregarious even with casual contacts.
- **Candor and Trust:** Americans generally place a high value on candor and on trust. We tend to be open and trustful and to accept others at face value.
- **Pride:** As Americans, we are proud of our phenomenal accomplishments in science, business, war, and world leadership. We tend to underestimate people from other cultures, including their ability to conduct successful intelligence operations against us.
- **Ambition:** Americans tend to be ambitious, oriented toward job advancement and professional recognition. Success is often measured by money and status.

These personality traits make many of us vulnerable to manipulation by people who offer friendship, understanding and flattery, or who offer opportunities for money or professional recognition, but who may have an ulterior motive for doing so.

4. Avoiding Intelligence Interest

To eliminate, or at least reduce, the possibility of your doing something inadvertent that may mark you as a person of special interest to one of these agencies, here are some DO NOT's to remember:

- DO NOT do anything which might be misconstrued or reflect poorly on your personal judgment, professional demeanor, or be embarrassing to you, your employer, or your country.
- DO NOT gossip about character flaws, financial problems, emotional relationships or marital difficulties of any co-workers, or yourself. This type of information is eagerly sought after by those who would like to exploit you or another employee.
- DO NOT carry, use, or purchase any narcotics, marijuana, or other abused drugs. Some countries have very stringent laws covering the import or use of medications and other substances. If you are using a prescribed medication that contains any narcotic substance or other medication that is subject to abuse, such as amphetamines or tranquilizers, carry a copy of the doctor's prescription for all medications and check for local restrictions and requirements prior to departure. Some countries may require additional documentation/certification from your doctor.
- DO NOT let a friendly ambiance and alcohol override your good sense and capacity when it comes to social drinking. In some countries, heavy drinking in the form of toasting is quite common, and very few westerners can keep up with a local national when it comes to drinking the national brew. If you are not careful, you could easily embarrass yourself, your employer, and/or your country. An accident while driving under the influence could lead to serious trouble.
- DO NOT engage in "black market" activities such as the illegal exchange of currency, or the purchase of religious icons or other local antiquities that may be stolen or otherwise not authorized for export.

4

- DO NOT accept or deliver letters, packages or anything else from or to anyone you do not know. You have no way of knowing what you are carrying and it could result in your being arrested for illegally importing a prohibited item.
- DO NOT engage in any type of political or religious activity, or carry any political or religious tracts or brochures, or publications likely to be offensive in the host country, such as pornography or weapons.
- DO NOT photograph anything that appears to be associated with the military or internal security of the country, including airports, ports, or restricted areas such as military installations.
- DO NOT ask the local government for any special favors or permits, such as permission to travel to a restricted area or a special benefit for a relative or friend.
- If in doubt, DO NOT.

5. Recognizing Intelligence Interest

Recognizing intelligence interest is discussed in *How Do I Know When I'm Being Targeted and Assessed?* Several scenarios that are particularly common while traveling abroad are mentioned here. The following situations should be closely scrutinized and usually avoided, if possible.

Repeated contacts with a local or third country national who is not involved in the business or other purpose of your visit, but who appears at each social or business function to which you are invited. This individual's demeanor may indicate more than just a passing interest in you or your work.

A close personal and social relationship with a foreign national of a hostile host government is often unavoidable for business reasons. In these instances, don't let your guard down. Don't assume that this is a true friendship.

Be skeptical of the accidental encounter with an unknown local national who strikes up a conversation and wants to practice English, talk about your country or your employment, buy you a drink because they have taken a liking to you, talk to you about politics, or who uses any other pretext to begin a "*friendly*" relationship. Do not accept events at their face value. Do not overlook a quick friendship or an apparent dispute. Evaluate the importance of events and do not judge them by their appearance.

If any of the above or anything else occurs which just does not ring true, be skeptical! It may be innocent, but exercise prudence and good judgment.

When you are out and about, be aware of your surroundings and be observant, without staring. When you enter a room, find out where the exits are and if possible, sit near an exit. If you become aware that you are under physical or technical surveillance, this is a strong indication that someone is interested in monitoring your activities and learning more about you. Physical surveillance refers to following you on foot or by car. The KGB in Moscow sometimes mobilized as many as 200 agents to surveille one suspected CIA officer. One trick used to determine if someone is following you is to casually drop something out of your pocket and observe who will pick it up.

Technical surveillance refers to bugging your hotel room, using a concealed camera to observe your behavior in your hotel room, or monitoring your phone calls.

Although obviously worrisome, surveillance is no cause for panic. It may be a routine search for information that can be used against you, initiated solely on the basis of the sensitive information to which you are presumed to have access. You may be followed only because you met with someone who happens to be under surveillance. The bug in your hotel room may be left over from a previous operation, or be a permanent installation that is activated only when the room is occupied by a more important target than you.

If you possess sensitive information, either in your head or in documents on your person, you should ASSUME that you may be followed and behave accordingly. Do not do or say anything that could be used against you or that might increase interest in you as a target. Although you should be alert at all times, DO NOT do anything that suggests you are either looking for or are trying to avoid surveillance. This would suggest that you are engaged in illegal or improper activities and make you an even more important target.

In your hotel room, ASSUME that the room and telephone are being monitored. DO NOT try to play investigator and start looking for electronic listening devices. This again could send the wrong signal to whoever is behind the surveillance. Just act normally and make sure that you do not say or do anything in your hotel room that you would not want to see printed on the front page of the local newspaper. And do not do or say anything that suggests you know or suspect someone is listening. Taunting the local security service is always wrong, as it is definitely counterproductive.

If you have any reason to believe that you are being targeted by an intelligence or security service or any criminal or terrorist group, there is only one course of action to follow. Report your suspicions to the American Embassy or Consulate or to your employer and follow their guidance. Report only to an American citizen, not to a local national. And report only in person, not by telephone, fax, or electronic mail, as such communications to the American Embassy or Consulate may be monitored.

6. Road to Recruitment

First of all, understand that Recruiting agents is the most dangerous task that a foreign intelligence agent can perform. They know that if they try and recruit the wrong person, they may be killed. If they are in the U.S.A., they will be imprisoned if caught.

That said, are you really a target for recruitment? How would you know? Foreign intelligence operatives are not obvious. They don't wear trench coats or have shifty eyes. In today's world, they're usually friendly people who pursue their trade under the guise of activities that appear normal and natural. They want to cultivate you as a *friend.* Trust no one.

The only thing you can be certain of is that you are a potential target if you have access to classified, controlled or sensitive proprietary information. That's why it's important to be careful what you say when talking with ANY foreign national.

Not just careful what you say about your work. Also, be careful what you say about yourself and your co-workers. Don't talk about the cost of putting two sons through college at the same time, or the cost of medical help for your daughter's leukemia. Don't talk about your stupid boss, how you hate the IRS, problems with your spouse, or your colleague's drinking problem. A foreign intelligence operative may interpret any of these as clues that you (or your colleague) may be worth cultivating.

You already know that you must report anything that suggests you may be the target of a foreign intelligence service or other hostile group. That sounds simple. What you may not realize is this: If you haven't learned how intelligence services operate, you very likely won't recognize when you are being targeted and assessed until the process is pretty far advanced. The purpose of this description of the "road to recruitment" -- is to help you recognize an intelligence operative even before he (or she) does anything overtly suspicious.

Foreign intelligence personnel look for any legitimate activity that lets them meet and gain some assessment of the people who have access to the information they want. They then become a part of this activity. The rituals of espionage like secret meetings and dead drops are often avoided, at least during the early stages of most cases.

If I'm trying to get information from you, my goal is to make it easy for you, not to give you sleepless nights. We meet over lunch, become friends. I learn what makes you tick, sympathize with your problems, and feed your ego. If it seems like you may be amenable, we talk about information that is easy for you to rationalize talking about. I look for ways to gain one small step of cooperation at a time. To gain your sympathy, I may talk about my country's need for economic development or the threat from my country's enemies. If it's done right, you may not know it's a spy operation until you are so far down the road that you are either afraid to turn back or don't want to turn back.

One of the most succinct descriptions of the spotting, assessment, development, and recruitment process used by all intelligence services was provided by a former Soviet KGB officer. He called it the "**road to recruitment**." While the terminology he used is typically Russian, the process is similar to that used by all intelligence services.

1,000 initial contacts leads to
100 operational contacts, which
leads to 10 developmental contacts,
which leads to 3 trusted sources,
which leads to
1 recruitment

Like a sales or marketing plan, the road to recruitment is a guide on how to proceed and what to expect. It is a gradual process of sorting through and winnowing down a large number of possibilities in order to succeed in eventually making just a few small sales (trusted sources) and perhaps one big one (full recruitment as an agent).

The foreign agent's goals at each stage on the road to recruitment are as follows:

Initial Contact: If not already known, he will confirm whether or not you have information of value. If you do have information of value, establish some logical basis for continuing contact and obtain your agreement to meet again. This is generally expected to be successful in about one out of ten cases. If you are known to them, bear in mind that the foreign intelligence service already knows a great deal about you: your financial condition (how much you earn, your net worth), where you live, where you went to school, your current job title and job description, your resume, your photograph, your family status, your religion, your position regarding the government, and your weaknesses and strengths. Scientific conferences, international business development programs, seminars, exhibits, and meetings of all types where networking is encouraged are spy heaven. They offer ideal opportunities for making a large number of initial contacts in a short period of time.

Operational Contact: Look for some indication of exploitable vulnerability or susceptibility. In other words, determine whether it's worth spending time and money developing the contact with you? The faster the foreign agent accomplishes this goal, the more time he/she has available to devote to promising developmental contacts. Again, the expectation of many intelligence collectors is to be successful in about one out of ten cases. One indicator of success is your willingness to talk about topics or people of intelligence interest. Elicitation of useful -- but not necessarily secret -- information is an interim goal, or way station, on the road to recruitment. Elicitation is discussed in greater detail in *Getting Information Out of Honest People Like Me*.

Developmental Contact: At this point, the goal is to establish a relationship of friendship and trust. Get to know what makes you tick as a person. Determine your weaknesses and your unfulfilled goals and ambitions. Give you some sense of personal interest or pleasure in maintaining the contact. Cause you to feel a sense of obligation. Start you down the road of providing information, beginning with easy and innocent requests for professional advice, discussion of developments in your professional field, discussion of your work colleagues and the best way to deal with them, your explanation of the rationale behind your company's policy or American government policy. This may progress to requests for articles from professional journals that are ostensibly difficult to get in your "*friend's*" home country or technical information about your company's products that is not protected but also not readily available. Anything to establish a regular pattern of your coming to meetings prepared to provide information, no matter how innocuous that information may be. A request for your organization's internal phone book is not innocuous. It's a red flag. For an intelligence organization, a phone book is a basic tool for identifying the names of people who have access to the key information their organization is seeking.

Trusted Source: Of each 10 developmental contacts, maybe three can be developed into trusted sources. These are regular sources of useful information. They are trusted in the sense that the foreign intelligence organization believes their source is telling the truth and is not reporting the contact to his/her security office. If a trusted source is providing classified information, it will usually be in oral discussions rather than in documentary form. A trusted source may not know (or not admit to themself) that their "*friend*" is an intelligence officer. Of every three trusted sources, perhaps only one will become fully recruited as a knowing agent who regularly provides classified documents or who accepts money in exchange for information or other services.

If you are the target, you should be reporting to your security officer by the time you are classified as an operational contact (being assessed). If you haven't reported it by the time you've graduated to a developmental contact, you may be close to getting into trouble. Your goal is to recognize this process and report it to your security officer. The foreign intelligence operative's goal is to make it so easy for you to get involved, or to put yourself in a compromising position, that you won't want to report or will be afraid to report it to your security officer.

Your main defense is awareness and reporting on your foreign contacts. If you report, your security officer can alert you when you are dealing with a known foreign intelligence operative, or he may identify a foreign intelligence operative as a result of your reporting. That's part of your security officer's job -- identifying the few intelligence officers or agents among the many legitimate government officials, businessmen, or scientists you meet. Your reports on your contacts are an important contribution to the data base that makes these identifications possible.

If the FBI or a military service counter-intelligence office learns about your contact, it will probably ask your security office if you are reporting on it. If you are not reporting it, they will be obliged to open an investigative case on <u>you</u>. In other words, if you do report, you are part of the solution. If you don't report, <u>you can become part of the problem</u>.

You should not avoid contact with foreigners or distrust all persons from abroad. Your encounters with foreign colleagues and cultures should be among your most treasured experiences. But you must be aware that among the millions of foreigners who come to our country, or whose countries you visit, there are some who would exploit your trust.

If you do find yourself in contact with a foreign intelligence operative, there's no need to be afraid -- only careful. You won't be hurt, but you may be manipulated and used -- if you let that happen. You are much more likely to be charmed by a "*friend*" than blackmailed by an enemy. In a case where the first foreign intelligence operative fails to develop a friendship with you, another foreign intelligence operative takes over after learning from the first about your weaknesses (motives that can be exploited) such as a love of money, opposition to the government or love of adventure.

If the contact goes so far that you are asked to provide information, perhaps as a "consultant," you should listen carefully, be observant, and remember as many details as possible. Keep all options open by neither agreeing nor refusing to cooperate. Remain calm, be noncommittal, ask for time, and report immediately to your security office.

The following tables examine in greater detail the first three stages on the road to recruitment. They look at it from the perspective of what you might observe as a target and what this means your contact might be trying to do.

Initial Contact

What You Observe	What It May Mean
Questions about the nature of your work at first meeting.	Trying to determine as rapidly as possible whether you are someone worth spending time on.
Invitation to lunch or any other request for follow-up meeting.	Test your willingness to maintain contact.
Make an erroneous statement about an activity or person that you are familiar with.	Trick you into providing the correct information, or test your willingness to do so.
Pretending or falsely implying to be a representative of a particular firm, organization or country.	A cover story to gain your confidence and make you more comfortable with the contact.
Unsolicited request for information via mail, phone, or Internet directed to you by name, rather than to other appropriate addressee such as corporate marketing department.	Collection of openly available information. Or testing your willingness to be helpful by responding to such a request, especially if request comes from a foreigner with the same national, ethnic, or religious background as you. If you respond, you may then be targeted and assessed by other means.

Operational Contact

What You Observe	What It May Mean
Discussions that lead in the direction of sensitive or classified topics.	Testing your willingness to talk about sensitive topics.
Inquiries about your own job satisfaction or professional rewards.	Looking for exploitable weaknesses, such as bitterness or alienation.
Talk about his/her country's need for economic development or threat from foreign enemies.	Elicit sympathy for his/her country's problems and motivate you to be helpful.
Requests for technical explanations from a person who, because of his or her alleged credentials, should already know the answer.	Getting you accustomed to responding to questions. Testing whether you respond to flattery about your knowledge or have a need to feel important. Or maybe the alleged credentials are not real.
Disclosure to you of what you would consider to be sensitive information.	Provoking you to verify facts or findings. Make you feel that it's okay to talk about such information. Trying to put contact on a "confidential" basis.
You are treated royally during foreign visit.	Developing a sense of obligation to somehow reciprocate. Setting the stage for relaxed discussion and further assessment.
Your advice is sought on subjects of common	Setting the precedent for you providing

| | information, no matter how innocuous it may be. Test whether flattery and making you feel important makes you more open and talkative. |
| interest. | |

Developmental Contact

What You Observe	What It May Mean
Offer of a consulting fee on a private basis, even for providing innocuous information.	Developing your financial motivation, getting you into the habit of providing information for money.
Request for introduction to another person, or to provide innocuous information such as unclassified reports from your library or an organizational telephone book, with no mention of compensation.	Testing your inclination to be helpful, or establishing a pattern of your providing information.
Attempts to get you inebriated while engaging in a technical discussion.	Trying to elicit privileged information, or testing whether you can be led into a compromising situation while drunk.
You receive expenses paid invitation to visit foreign country to attend conference, share technical expertise, or for sabbatical.	The invitation may be entirely innocent, but if the intelligence service arranged it you may be in an advanced developmental stage. The goal may be to reward you for your assistance, create a sense of obligation, or get you on their home turf where they can try to compromise you by heavy drinking, black market currency exchange, or sexual provocation.
Attempts to gain inside or privileged information by offering favors or money.	This is past the assessment and development stage, moving toward recruitment.

If you are targeted and assessed by a foreign intelligence officer, this certainly does not mean that you have done anything wrong. It does not in any way reflect on your reliability. You are a natural target because of your access to protected information, and because your job or other circumstances brings you into contact with foreign nationals. You have done nothing wrong unless you start maintaining a regular contact without reporting it to your security officer.

7. Getting Information Out of Honest People Like Me

Methods of Operation

This section discusses methods that foreign intelligence services, foreign corporations and other intelligence collectors use to obtain protected information of both a military and civilian nature.

Some of these methods are entirely legal. We don't distinguish between legal and illegal methods, because the same foreign intelligence services, corporations and other intelligence collectors frequently employ both legal and illegal methods in a coordinated effort. Both types of methods can have the same damaging result -- loss of a technological edge in either military weapons or the global marketplace.

Moreover, the distinction between legal and illegal is itself sometimes questionable. For example, there is no law against stealing discarded documents from your organization's dumpster or from a trash container outside your home. Until 1996, the United States did not even have a law against industrial espionage.

8. Contact with Foreign Relatives

Contact with foreign relatives, or other persons in foreign countries to whom you have ties of affection, influence, or obligation, can be a security concern -- especially if those persons are in a country known to conduct intelligence operations against the United States. The greater your value as an intelligence target, the more likely these persons will be exploited to gain information about you. The more vulnerable they are to coercion, exploitation, or pressure (for example, they work for the government or are dependent upon the government in any other way), the more likely they are to be used for this purpose.

The likelihood that a foreign security or intelligence service will develop interest in you may be increased by actions you take that draw the service's attention to your ties of affection for or obligation to one of its citizens. This includes regular mail or telephone contact, sending packages or money or medicine, or visiting a foreign relative or associate. The more frequent and extensive the contact, or the stronger the apparent ties of affection or obligation, the greater the chances that the contact will come to the attention of and be exploited by the foreign security or intelligence service.

If the foreign security or intelligence service identifies you as a target, they may seek to assess your vulnerabilities and gradually draw you into a web of compromising circumstances. Indications that such a process may be underway include:

- Suspected delay or tampering with mail to or from foreign correspondents.
- Suspected monitoring of telephone calls to or from foreign relatives or associates.
- Discreet or official inquiries to the foreign relative or associate about you.
- Any unusual contact with police or security authorities during foreign travel, especially foreign officials contacting you under any pretext while you are visiting with relatives in the foreign country.
- The foreign relative or associate advising you of any type of difficulty with local authorities, or asking for money or medicine under circumstances that seem the least bit unusual.

If a foreign intelligence or security service can manipulate you into sending or transporting money, medicine, or goods to a foreign relative, this confirms your sense of obligation to help the relative. If you send or transport the money, medicine, or goods through illegal channels, the relative is subject to arrest and, therefore, vulnerable to duress. If you can be made to believe the relative's problems with the authorities are your fault, this creates an even greater sense of obligation. If you send money, medicine, or gifts through illegal channels, the security service also has a basis for detaining and questioning you during your visit to that country. If you fail to report such developments to U.S. security authorities, you take the first step on a path toward concealing a relationship with a foreign intelligence or security service.

9. Bugging Hotel Rooms

It is sometimes said that "All hotel rooms abroad are bugged for audio and visual surveillance." Of course, it is not true that all of them are bugged, but a great many are -- especially in major hotels frequented by foreign business and government travelers. To maintain an adequate level of security awareness while conducting business abroad, you must operate on the assumption that your hotel room conversations are being monitored. If you are an active target who is known to pick up local women, you could also be filmed by a concealed camera.

The goal of surreptitious monitoring may be to learn your business or negotiating strategy, identify your local contacts, assess your vulnerabilities, or obtain evidence that can be used to accuse you of improper activities or to pressure you to cooperate.

It is noteworthy that legal restrictions against technical surveillance that apply in the United States have not been adopted by other countries with which we have close trading ties. The overseas operations of American companies engaged in international commerce are particularly vulnerable.

Most foreign security and intelligence services have various means of screening incoming visitors to identify persons of potential intelligence interest. They also have well-established contacts with the hotels that commonly host conferences and meetings with international participation. For convenience, some even maintain permanent offices within the largest hotels. If the local intelligence service considers you a significant intelligence target, it may arrange for you to be assigned a room that is already prepared for the desired monitoring.

Some luxury hotels offer a baby monitoring service to guests who wish to use the club or guest services, while still minding the toddlers asleep in their hotel room. This service is an integral part of the hospitality features incorporated into the hotel phone system. That means it is possible from a central location to activate the microphone within the telephone set within any room at any time. Consider how this might be used by the local security service.

Even without such a built-in system, it takes only a minute or two for someone to enter a hotel room and bug the telephone so that all room conversations can be monitored from a line connected to the hotel switchboard.

10. Theft While Traveling

Your information and valuables are far more vulnerable to theft while traveling abroad than in the United States. Principal targets for theft include:

- Government and business documents of interest to the local intelligence service.

Personal documents (passport and other ID and travel documents) of interest to criminal organizations, including those that arrange illegal immigration to the U.S.

- Laptop computers are of interest to everyone -- for the information on them, for resale, or for personal use.
- Expensive jewelry, cameras, and any other items that are easy to sell.

You have special vulnerabilities in your hotel room, elsewhere in your hotel, while in the airport or on the train, with sensitive equipment in transit, and in any office to which local foreign nationals have unrestricted access.

11. Hotel Rooms and Vaults

"Bag operations" is the term commonly used to describe surreptitious entry into hotel rooms to steal, photograph, or photocopy documents; steal or copy magnetic media; or download from laptop computers. Bag operations are common. In fact, they are routine procedure in quite a few countries.

Bag operations are typically conducted by the host government's security or intelligence service, frequently with cooperation of the hotel staff. Hotel security staffs commonly maintain close contact with the local police and government security service. It is common for retired government security and intelligence officers to obtain employment in the security offices of major hotels and corporations. Bag operations may also be conducted by the corporation you are dealing with or by a competitor company. They may be done during the day while you are out of the room or at night while you are asleep. Yes, they do take the risk of coming into your room while you are sleeping!

Government and business travelers often report that their belongings have been searched while they were absent from their hotel room. In some cases, they have returned to their room soon after departing, to retrieve a forgotten item, and find persons in their room claiming they are there to repair a broken TV, etc. Seldom is anything missing; the purpose is only to copy documents or download information from a traveler's laptop computer. Sometimes there is little effort to conceal the search. Other times it is more subtle. If done correctly, the traveler will not be aware of the search.

Leaving sensitive government or company information in your hotel room, even in a locked briefcase or the safe provided in your room, is an invitation for material to be copied or photographed while you are out. Hotel vaults are not much better. In most cases, foreign intelligence officers can gain access to hotel lockboxes or vaults without you becoming aware of the compromise.

Never leave a laptop computer with sensitive information on it in the room unattended. Keep it in your personal possession at all times or don't take it on the trip. If you must take a laptop, use encryption to protect sensitive files and perform regular backups to ensure no loss of vital information in case of theft.

Suitcase and attaché case locks may delay the trained professional for a few minutes but will not protect your sensitive information. Nevertheless, it is wise to keep your luggage locked whenever you are out of the room. Although locks will not inhibit the professional thief or intelligence agent, they will keep the curious maid honest. Curious hotel employees are even more likely to remain honest if combination locks are set so that the combination for each piece of luggage is different. For attaché cases with two combination locks, use different combinations for each lock.

The only solution to the security problem is to take as little sensitive information as possible when traveling overseas, and to carry what you must take on your person, possibly on computer media. Computer diskettes and CD-ROMs must also be carried with you at all times.

If you must carry sensitive information, the following suggestions may be helpful.

While asleep or in the shower, engage both the dead bolt and the privacy latch or chain on the hotel room door. A hotel's emergency keys can override the dead bolt locks, so the latch or chain is your principal source of security. (Note: Many hotel rooms have a door to a connecting room. This is a potential vulnerability, as these doors do not normally have a privacy latch or chain.) Utilize a portable or improvised burglar alarm while asleep. Two ash trays and a water glass are quite effective as an alarm when placed on the floor in front of the door into your room. Place a water glass in one ashtray and balance the second ashtray on top of the glass. If a straight chair is available, place it next to the door and put the ash tray/water glass alarm on the edge of the chair where it will fall with enough racket to wake you.

When leaving the room, make a mental or written note of how your suitcase or other personal property that would not normally be touched by the cleaning personnel was left. Any movement might suggest that others were in the room to examine your belongings. The same procedure is even more effective to check for surreptitious entry while you were asleep.

Jewelry or other valuables should normally be left at home, but you may need to protect a substantial amount of money. Guidelines for protecting money from thieves are different from those for protecting sensitive information from the local intelligence or security service. Money should not be kept on your person. It should be kept in a safe in a local office or in the hotel's safe deposit box or safe. This is safer than a room safe and may also make the hotel liable for any loss. Liability laws in many countries provide that the hotel is not liable for the loss of guest property unless it is in the "care, custody and control of the hotel." Additional protection may be gained by double enveloping all valuables, initialing across the seams, and then taping all edges and seams (over the initials).

If you determine that an item is missing, conduct a thorough search prior to reporting the incident to hotel security. Do not expect to receive a copy of the security report, as it is an internal document. The incident should be reported to the local police, the security officer at the nearest U.S. Embassy or Consulate, and your insurance carrier. Hotel security can provide a letter verifying that you reported property missing.

12. Elsewhere in the Hotel

There are a number of areas of your hotel where you are particularly vulnerable to theft.

Rest Rooms: Female travelers should be careful about placing purses on hangers on the inside of the lavatory doors or on the floor in stalls -- two frequent locations for grab and run thefts. On occasion, unauthorized persons use rest rooms for other types of theft or to deal drugs or engage in prostitution.

Public Telephones: Areas around public telephones are often used by criminals to stage pickpocket activity or theft. Keep briefcases and purses in view or "in touch" while using phones. Safeguard your telephone credit card numbers. Criminals sometimes hang around public telephones to gather credit card numbers and then sell the numbers for unauthorized use.

Hotel Bars and Restaurants: Purse snatchers and briefcase thieves are known to work hotel bars and restaurants waiting for unknowing guests to drape these items on chairs or under tables, only to discover them missing as they are departing. Keep items in view or "in touch". Be alert to scams involving an unknown person spilling a drink or food on your clothing. An accomplice may be preparing to steal your wallet, briefcase or purse.

Pool or Beach Areas: These are fertile areas for thieves to take advantage of guests enjoying recreation. Leave valuables in the hotel. Safeguard your room key and camera. Sign for food and beverages on your room bill rather than carry cash.

Prostitutes take advantage of travelers around the world through various ploys, including use of "knock out" drugs and theft from the victim's room. Avoid engaging persons you do not know and refrain from inviting them to your guest room.

13. Airports and Trains

Airports, railroad terminals and trains are easy targets for pickpockets, thieves, and terrorist bombers. Unattended baggage is an obvious risk. Checked baggage is also at risk and should never contain valuables such as a camera or sensitive papers. It is not unusual for government and business travelers to report broken suitcase locks and rearranged contents.

Theft from sleeping compartments on trains is surprisingly common. Train thieves spray chemicals inside sleeping compartments to render the occupant(s) unconscious in order to enter and steal valuables. Using this technique, valuables can be stolen from under a sleeping person's pillow. A locked door may be helpful but is no guarantee.

Laptop computers are a prime target for theft everywhere, but they are especially vulnerable in airports. They are stolen for the value of the information on them as well as for the value of the computer.

According to Safeware, an insurer of personal computers, 10% of all laptop thefts occur in airports. Airports offer an inviting atmosphere for thieves due to large crowds, hectic schedules, and weary travelers. Laptop thefts commonly occur in places where people set them down -- at security checkpoints, pay phones, lounges and restaurants, check-in lines, and restrooms. Two incidents at separate European airports demonstrate the modus operandi of thieves operating in pairs to target laptop computers:

Airport security at Brussels International Airport reported that two thieves exploited a contrived delay around the security X-ray machines. The first thief preceded the traveler through the security checkpoint and then loitered around the area where security examines carry-on luggage. When the traveler placed his laptop computer onto the conveyer belt of the X-ray machine, the second thief stepped in front of the traveler and set off the metal detector. With the traveler now delayed, the first thief removed the traveler's laptop from the conveyer belt just after it passed through the X-ray machine and quickly disappeared.

While walking around the Frankfurt International Airport in Germany, a traveler carrying a laptop computer in his roll bag did not notice a thief position himself to walk in front of him. The thief stopped abruptly as the traveler bypassed a crowd of people, causing the traveler also to stop. A second thief, who was following close behind, quickly removed the traveler's laptop computer from his roll bag and disappeared into the crowd.

All travelers, both domestic and international, should be alert to any sudden diversions when traveling, especially when transiting transportation terminals. If victimized, travelers should report the thefts immediately to the authorities and be able to provide the makes, model information, and serial numbers of their laptop computers, or any other items of value.

14. Sensitive Equipment in Transit

Sensitive equipment may be stolen so that it can be copied through reverse engineering. For some purposes, it may be sufficient to only gain access to the equipment for a brief period.

For example, a cleared company participated in an air show that took place overseas. The company shipped over an operational $250,000 multi-mode radar system that can be used on fighter aircraft. At the conclusion of the air show, the radar system was packaged for return shipping by company personnel, and the radar assembly was actually bolted to the shipping container. The shipping container was routed through a third country with the customs seals intact.

Upon being opened by company personnel, it was discovered that the radar was no longer bolted to the shipping container. As a result, the radar system was damaged beyond repair. It was determined that the radar was properly bolted down at the time it was prepared for shipment. It also was determined that the country that sponsored the air show was keenly interested in the radar's technology. It is not known whether the intruder's failure to re-bolt the radar was an oversight or was done deliberately to destroy evidence of whatever was done to examine the radar.

Lesson learned: The company did not really need to take the entire radar assembly to the air show. A mock-up without the internal mechanisms could have been set up along with photographs of the internal components.

15. Overseas Communications

Many foreign telecommunications companies are owned or controlled by the government. Even those not government-owned or controlled are regulated by the government and will normally cooperate when their government requests assistance in monitoring specific lines.

Under these circumstances, it is easy to intercept and monitor telephone, fax, e-mail, computer, and any other form of electronic communications. A typical communications monitoring scenario might be as follows:

A foreign intelligence service rents an office near the targeted office or home or in another location selected to provide easy access to telecommunications facilities or transmissions from the target.

An electronic listening post is set up in the office and manned around the clock. The listening post eavesdrops on telephone, fax, telex, and computer communications. Computers screen all communications and pick out those that are potentially valuable by identifying key words such as the name of a company, person, technology, product, project, or anything else that may identify a topic of interest to the monitoring organization or its customers. Interesting communications are recorded and screened manually for the preparation of written reports. In many countries, a principal goal is to support national businesses by providing them with information on such things as their foreign competitors' technology, marketing plans, prices, bids, and negotiating strategies.

Government programs to intercept foreign telecommunications are now standard practice in many countries. Global economic competition, the great increase in global telecommunications, and the development of computer search engines to screen massive amounts of electronic material make it cost-effective for an increasing number of countries to develop extensive intercept programs.

The cost and technology for developing a significant intercept capability is now well within the capability of many corporations, criminal syndicates, or terrorist groups in addition to foreign governments. The equipment for this can be obtained easily by almost anyone.

Security Countermeasures

You must assume that all overseas telecommunications that would be valuable to another government, company, or group will be intercepted, recorded, organized into reports, and reviewed by the persons for whom that information has value. Although that will not be true in every case, the likelihood is sufficiently great that you cannot afford to assume otherwise if compromise of the information would be a significant loss. In most cases, it is virtually impossible to detect when telecommunications are being intercepted and monitored.

This leaves three alternatives:

- Encrypt all telecommunications that you cannot afford to have compromised. However, some countries do not allow encryption of telecommunications traffic within their borders.
- Communicate by courier.
- Accept the loss of confidentiality and plan accordingly.

Access to telephones, fax machines and computers should be controlled to reduce the possibility of tampering. Telephones can be adjusted so that they act as transmitters even after they are hung up. Conversations near a phone may be transmitted to the foreign country's phone system switching facility and can be monitored from anywhere between the phone and that facility. Computers and fax machines can be tampered with to facilitate monitoring that bypasses the encryption system.

Security procedures should be followed carefully when operating any computer linked to an outside network or telephone system.

16. What to Do If Arrested

Foreign police and intelligence agencies can detain persons for many reasons, or for no reason other than suspicion or curiosity. In some countries where security organs have sweeping powers to detain persons believed to be a threat to national security, virtually any government document or official statistic falls under the definition of "state secret." American standards of what is "open information" do not apply in many foreign countries.

If arrested, follow these guidelines.

- Ask to contact the nearest American Embassy or Consulate. As a citizen of another country, you have this right; but that does not mean that your hosts will allow you to exercise that right. If you are refused or just ignored, continue to make the request periodically until they accede and let you contact the embassy or consulate.
- Stay calm, maintain your dignity and do not do anything to provoke the arresting officer(s). Do not admit anything or volunteer any information.
- Do not sign anything. Often, part of the detention procedure is to ask or tell the detainee to sign a written report. Decline politely until such time as the document is examined by an attorney or an embassy/consulate representative.
- Do not accept anyone on face value. When the embassy or consulate representative arrives, request some identification before discussing your situation.
- Do not fall for the ruse of helping the ones who are detaining you in return for your release. They can be very imaginative in their proposals on how you can be of assistance to them. Do not sell yourself out by agreeing to anything. If they will not take no for an answer, do not make a firm commitment or sign anything. Tell them that you will think it over and let them know. Once out of their hands, contact the American Embassy or Consulate for protection and assistance in getting out of the country.

17. Who's Doing What to Whom?

America's role as the dominant political, economic, and military force in the world makes it the Number 1 target for foreign espionage. As FBI Director Louis Freeh reported to Congress, foreign intelligence activities against the United States have grown in diversity and complexity since the end of the Cold War.

In addition to the intelligence services of friendly as well as unfriendly countries, sources of the threat to classified and other protected information include:

- Foreign or multinational corporations.
- Foreign government-sponsored educational and scientific institutions.
- Free-lance agents (some of whom are unemployed former intelligence officers).
  Computer hackers.
- Terrorist organizations.
  Revolutionary groups.
- Extremist ethnic or religious
  organizations. Drug syndicates.
- Organized crime.

The intelligence services of friendly and allied countries are now more active in intelligence operations against the United States than during the Cold War. Espionage by friends in addition to adversaries has long been more widespread than generally realized. For example:

During the past 20 years, Americans have been arrested and convicted of spying for South Korea, Taiwan, Philippines, Israel, Greece, Saudi Arabia, Iraq, Jordan, Ghana, Liberia, South Africa, El Salvador and Ecuador -- in addition to Russia, the former Soviet Union, China, and the various formerly communist countries.

In many cases, foreign targets in this country have not changed. "There is still a deadly serious interest in 'traditional' intelligence activities such as penetrating the U.S. intelligence community, collecting classified information on U.S. military defense systems, and purloining the latest advances in our country's science and technology sector."

In a world that increasingly measures national power and national security in economic terms, foreign countries and corporations are placing increased emphasis on the collection of scientific, technical and economic-related information of all types. The increasing value of trade secrets in the global and domestic marketplaces, and the corresponding spread of technology, have combined to significantly increase both the opportunities and the incentives for conducting economic espionage, as discussed in Economic Collection and Industrial Espionage. The illegal export of controlled technology is a related but somewhat different offense discussed in Illegal Technology Transfer.

Important changes in the international economic environment and technological advances have increased our vulnerability to some types of foreign intelligence operations.

The development of a global economy, with a rapid expansion in foreign trade, travel, and personal relationships of all kinds, now makes it easier than ever before for foreign intelligence officers or agents of foreign corporations to establish personal contact with and assess Americans with access to valuable classified, controlled, or proprietary information. As international contacts have become more common, it has become easier for foreign intelligence officers and agents to contact, assess and develop targets without arousing suspicion.

Computer networks and other developments in the information revolution increase exponentially the amount of damage that can be done by a single insider who betrays his or her trust.

The National Security Threat List guides the FBI's counter-intelligence strategy for protection against these threats.

18. Overseas Offices

Offices of U.S. Government agencies and U.S. businesses in foreign countries are vulnerable both to burglary and to theft of information by local national employees.

For example, the Western European office of a large American corporation was burglarized in an obvious case of industrial espionage. Located on the sixth floor of a 12-story office building, it was entered from the outside window ledge by breaking the window. The thieves ignored the company's expensive computers and other valuable items and went directly to their target -- the company's marketing and business data, client and business contact lists, and banking information. Wastebaskets can be a great source of information.

Foreign offices of U.S. Government and business organizations are staffed, in part, by local citizens. In many countries, some of these employees cooperate voluntarily with the local security or intelligence service or are pressured or coerced into doing so.

In one allied Western European country, collecting proprietary information from the offices of American and other foreign corporations with offices in that country is known as "economic patriotism." Collected information is provided routinely to local competitors of the U.S. companies. In many countries, local national employees are also debriefed for assessment data about the American personnel.

Foreign intelligence interest is not necessarily determined by an employee's rank in the company. Researchers, key business managers, and corporate executives can all be targets, but so can support employees such as secretaries, computer operators, technicians, and maintenance people. The latter frequently have good, if not the best, access to competitive information. Additionally, their lower pay and rank may provide fertile ground for manipulation by an intelligence agency.

Protection of sensitive information is very difficult under these circumstances. Discussion of all the physical and technical security requirements for protection of proprietary technologies and sensitive commercial information is beyond the scope of this security guide.

19. Foreign Travel Incidents Identified by Counter-intelligence Officials

Method	Incidents
Elicitation of sensitive or classified information from travelers	During unclassified presentations in a non-sensitive country, a traveler had to deflect several questions from host country nationals that touched on sensitive or classified information. At one presentation, he was asked questions about a specific nuclear isotope and its relation to U.S. nuclear devices.
	While on a trip to a "sensitive" country to present a class, a traveler reported that host country officials questioned him on sensitive subjects.
Offers of sexual favors to travelers	A traveler to a "sensitive" country admitted to extensive sexual contact with various women, including two female employees at the facility where he was visiting. A laboratory counter-intelligence official was particularly concerned about these activities because of the potential for blackmail.
Surveillance of travelers' movements	A traveler to a "sensitive" country noticed that his room had translucent disks on the walls and motion detectors in the ceilings. The traveler believed that these devices held technical surveillance equipment.
	Travelers to a "sensitive" country noted that three times the number of security officers were assigned to their group as in the past. These security officers were present at all meetings, escorted the travelers everywhere, reviewed all E-mails and phone calls, and monitored side conversations during the meetings.
Searches of travelers' hotel room and belongings	A traveler to a "sensitive" country for several days of meetings found, on returning to his hotel room after an overnight outing, that a tamper-indicating seal on his computer was broken, although the computer system was still locked. Also, he noted other instances, including the observed entry into the hotel room of a third traveler.
	While staying at a guest house, a traveler to a "sensitive" country noted, when he returned to his room, that his belongings and papers were out of order and sloppily put back in different places. In addition, someone had attempted to access his hand-held electronic organizer.
Electronic interception of telecommunication systems	During a traveler's telephone call from a "sensitive" country to his wife, the wife mentioned that she would be playing bingo on a bus trip. A short time later in the hotel lounge, someone mentioned to the traveler the bingo trip that his wife had talked about. The next day, another person asked, "What is bingo?"
Eavesdropping on or recording of travelers' activities with audio and visual devices	During a meeting in a "sensitive" country, the host country individual responsible for the administration and logistics of the discussions walked in the room; pounded and pushed on one of the wooden wall panels, which opened up and exposed a mass of video cameras, tapes, and electronic equipment; and replaced the tapes on the machines.
	A traveler in a U.S. delegation to a "sensitive" country said that before the start of one of its meetings, the delegation met in private

	to discuss talking points, negotiation strategies, and issues it wanted to avoid with its hosts. When the meetings began, the host country chairman began listing, almost point-by-point, each of the issues that the delegation had discussed—almost exactly mirroring the U.S. position.
Monitoring of travelers' conversations and behavior through interpreters	On the last day of a workshop in a "sensitive" country, a host country national gave a set of postcards to a traveler depicting scenes of a nearby city. The traveler had never mentioned to this individual his interest in visiting this city. However, he had mentioned this interest to an interpreter at the conference earlier in the week.

20. In the Line of Fire: American Travelers Abroad

While traveling abroad, you are on the other country's home turf, where the local security and intelligence services have many resources available. They can monitor and, to some extent, control the environment in which you live and do your work. As an American government official, scientist, or business traveler with access to useful information, you can become a target of the local intelligence or security service in almost any country.

Some of the activities that may be directed against you will be quite sophisticated, and you are unlikely to notice them or to identify them for what they are. Others may be crude and obvious, like most of those described below.

This section consists of a series of anecdotes about foreign intelligence activities observed by travelers from the Department of Energy's Lawrence Livermore, Los Alamos, Sandia, and Oak Ridge National Laboratories. Most of the travelers were scientists traveling overseas on official business to attend meetings and conferences and to perform research. They were traveling in countries that place a high priority on collecting information about U.S. technology.

The U.S. Government, as a matter of policy, does not identify publicly which foreign countries represent the greatest intelligence threat. To do so would create a false sense of security when dealing with any of the unnamed countries. The reality is that most technologically advanced or developing countries, including some democratic countries that are closely allied with or supported by the United States, place a high priority on acquiring U.S. technology by both fair means and foul.

The anecdotes below are a typical sample of observations reported over, and over, and over again by government, business, scientific, and academic travelers. In some countries, such happenings are rather normal, not exceptional. By reporting your observations to your security office, you make it possible for your security office to keep abreast of what is happening and to warn you and others, before you travel, about things you might encounter during your trip.

Anecdotes

A traveler in a U.S. delegation said that before the start of one of its meetings, the delegation met in private to discuss talking points, negotiation strategies, and issues it wanted to avoid with its hosts. When the meetings began, the host country chairman began his opening remarks and listed almost point-by-point each of the issues that the delegation had discussed. Because no host country nationals had been privy to the delegation's discussions, the traveler was convinced that the discussions must have been monitored.

A traveler awoke in his hotel room and realized he was late for a meeting with his team members. On the way out of his room, he saw an unidentified male standing in the open doorway of a team member's room. The male turned toward the traveler and said something in the native language to someone else in the room. Immediately, a woman stepped out of the room and into the hall. Both individuals appeared very surprised and nervous about being discovered. The traveler relayed this incident to the team, none of whom had experienced any problems. The team member whose room had been entered possessed all the financial data that the U.S. team was going to use in the negotiations. The host country would be very interested in obtaining that information.

A traveler attending a workshop returned to his hotel room after being away for dinner. He went to bed and was awakened six hours later by a beeping noise. The noise was coming from the traveler's laptop computer. The computer cover was closed, but the unit was not shut off. The traveler believes that while he was out of the room, it was searched and the laptop was opened but not turned off. This caused the battery to run down, which is what had caused the beeping. The traveler had not turned on the computer during his trip. No classified, sensitive, or proprietary information was on the computer's hard drive. On the last night of the workshop, a banquet was held, and a considerable amount of alcohol was consumed by participants.
However, one host country participant was observed to be drinking no more than an ounce or two all night. Later, this individual offered to provide a woman for the traveler and another colleague. Both declined.

During a workshop, a traveler was approached by a host country national who addressed the traveler by name before the traveler had a chance to put on his name tag. Throughout this week of meetings, this individual was very attentive to the U.S. travelers. He was interested in learning about the traveler's laboratory address and how the traveler's organization in the laboratory was related to other laboratory programs.

A traveler found four entries for "guest access" on his laptop computer. The computer had been locked with a commercially available padlock and left in his room unattended. It was not clear if someone had actually accessed any files on the hard drive. He then checked the computer's protection software and found another "guest entry" had been logged on. The date of this entry coincided with a previous trip the traveler took to the same country.

A traveler telephoned his wife at home. During their conversation, his wife mentioned an upcoming bus trip that she would be taking and that they would be playing bingo on the bus. A short time later, someone mentioned to the traveler the bingo trip that his wife had talked about. The next day, another person asked, "What is bingo?"

A traveler presented various lectures to university audiences and the general public throughout the country. Although the presentations were all unclassified, the traveler had to deflect several questions from host country nationals at each venue that touched on sensitive or classified information. At one lecture, he was asked questions about a specific nuclear isotope and its relation to U.S. nuclear devices.

A traveler was propositioned by prostitutes every night. On the first night, he received a phone call from a prostitute within a few minutes of entering his hotel room. This was the case each night, and he did not think it was the same woman every night. He declined these offers. On one occasion, a prostitute knocked on his hotel door. The traveler said that there was a female "hall monitor" in the hotel. He believed that the monitor was providing surveillance for prostitutes.

In a moment of frustration, a traveler mentioned to another traveler while in his hotel room that "any decent hotel would at least have a spare roll of toilet paper in each room." Later that day, upon returning to the hotel room, the traveler noticed that there was an additional roll of toilet paper in his room. This and other unusual occurrences during the visit led the traveler to believe that audio surveillance was being utilized.

While engaged in negotiations in another country, a laboratory team reported that the host nation participants were very forceful in trying to have a particular technology included in the contract's statement of work. This technology currently cannot be shared and thus was not included in the statement of work.

A traveler noticed that his laptop computer had been tampered with while it was left unattended in the closet of his hotel room. When he turned on the computer, he noticed that someone had successfully bypassed and turned off the password protection. The battery compartment door on the underside of the computer was broken. The traveler reported that one of his colleagues had a similar problem with his laptop.

A traveler reported that a colleague placed something in his suitcase that would alert him if the suitcase was searched during his absence. Later, the suitcase was searched, but nothing was taken from it.

A traveler was invited to join a high-ranking official on a hunting trip for the weekend. The traveler told the official that he had been briefed and instructed to always bring along another team member when traveling in that country. The official told him he could bring along his host country's interpreter. The traveler did not go on the hunting trip.

While staying at a guest house, a traveler placed his belongings on the shelves in the room. He carefully placed his business paperwork between various clothing items. Several hours later, when he returned to his room, he noticed that someone had gone through his papers, because they were out of order and sloppily put back in different places. Also, someone attempted to access his electronic organizer.

A traveler was approached by an interpreter with questions about his personal life. The traveler was not comfortable with these questions and refused to answer them.

A traveler suspected that the briefcase he had left in his hotel room had been tampered with. His briefcase, which he never locked during the trip, was found locked when he tried to open it. The briefcase contained nothing sensitive or classified, and nothing appeared to be missing.

A traveler reported that the interpreter from the host country appeared to be compiling biographical information on him. The interpreter said that he recognized the traveler from an article in a trade magazine, which the traveler found unlikely.

An individual who was not from the host country asked a traveler questions about his new work at his laboratory. The traveler was surprised by this question, because few people knew of his new assignment, and this was not related to the purpose of his travel. The traveler said that it seemed the individual was specifically assigned to him to elicit information. The traveler did not provide the requested information.

A traveler experienced a burglary in his second-floor hotel room. The traveler's briefcase was taken, but other valuables, including money left next to the briefcase, were not taken. The briefcase contained documents with proprietary and sensitive information, the traveler's laboratory identification badge, and his office key. The briefcase was later recovered and returned to the traveler with all the contents intact by a host country colleague.

A traveler at an international conference was approached by another participant who asked for a list of fission products. The traveler thought this participant was asking about fission products released from nuclear reactors and said these were available in the open literature. The participant then said that he wanted products from nuclear weapons. The traveler told him that he did not work in that area. The participant then asked for the names of people who do work in that area.

At a meeting that was held in a hotel, housekeepers entered the conference room and rearranged some of the plants, placing one plant very close to the traveler and another U.S. laboratory colleague. Their host joked that they could not hear them well enough and so moved the plant closer. The traveler presumed that the plan contained a bug.

21. Antiterrorism and Force Protection

Introduction

This Antiterrorism section should be read in association with the Risks During Foreign Travel module. The latter deals with the protection of sensitive information and routine safety procedures during foreign travel. This section deals more specifically with the protection of people from terrorist attack, especially people on duty assignment abroad.

Department of Defense (DoD) policy requires that all DoD military and civilian personnel and supporting defense contractors receive an Antiterrorism/Force Protection (AT/FP) briefing before travel to any destination outside the United States (except Guam and Midway Island). DoD contractors are to provide their personnel working on contracts outside the United States with AT/FP awareness information commensurate with that which DoD provides to its military and civilian personnel and their families.

This Antiterrorism section is intended to meet the DoD requirements for such a briefing. If the travel is to a moderate, significant or high-threat area, DoD requires that the AT/FP briefing be supplemented by a recent update on threats in the specific area of travel. Updated threat information on specific countries is readily available from the State Department. On the Internet, go http://travel.state.gov, then click on Travel Warnings and Consular Information Sheets. Country-specific threat information is also available from the State Department by telephone at (202) 647-5225 or by fax at (202) 647-3000.

For additional information on DOD policy and procedures, see the Department of Defense antiterrorism assistance web site at http://www.dtic.mil/jcs/force_protection. This site includes links to CINC/Theater-specific requirements.

Although antiterrorism training cannot guarantee your safety, it will make you more aware of your surroundings, help you avoid becoming a terrorist target, and improve your chances of emerging unharmed if you do become a target.

The Department of Defense (DoD) defines "antiterrorism" as "*defensive* measures used to reduce the vulnerability of individuals and property to terrorist acts." This is distinct from "counterterrorism," which refers to "*offensive* measures taken to prevent, deter, and respond to terrorism." Both are part of the DoD concept of "force protection," which brings together all the security disciplines in a broader program to protect service members, civilian employees, family members, facilities and equipment.

The Department of Defense uses a standardized set of terms to describe the Terrorism Threat Level in each country. These terms are Low, Moderate, Significant, and High. The Defense Intelligence Agency sets the Terrorism Threat Level for each country based on analysis of all available information.

Commanders at all levels use the DIA Terrorism Threat Level plus their own threat analyses as a basis for developing plans and programs to protect assets within their area of responsibility. These are called Force Protection Conditions. A Force Protection Conditions is a set of specific security measures promulgated by the commander after considering a variety of factors including the threat level, current events that might increase the risk, observed suspicious activities, etc.

There is a graduated series of Force Protection Conditions ranging from Force Protection Conditions Normal to Force Protection Conditions Delta. There is a process by which commanders at all levels can raise or lower the Force Protection Conditions based on local conditions, specific threat information and/or guidance from higher headquarters. The four Force Protection Conditions above normal are:

Force Protection Conditions ALPHA--This condition applies when there is a general threat of possible terrorist activity against personnel and facilities, the nature and extent of which are unpredictable, and circumstances do not justify full implementation of Force Protection Conditions BRAVO measures. The measures in this Force Protection Conditions must be capable of being maintained indefinitely.

Force Protection Conditions BRAVO--This condition applies when an increased and more predictable threat of terrorist activity exists. The measures in this Force Protection Conditions must be capable of being maintained for weeks without causing undue hardship, affecting operational capability, and aggravating relations with local authorities.

Force Protection Conditions CHARLIE--This condition applies when an incident occurs or intelligence is received indicating some form of terrorist action against personnel and facilities is imminent. Implementation of measures in this Force Protection Conditions for more than a short period probably will create hardship and affect the peacetime activities of the unit and its personnel.

Force Protection Conditions DELTA--This condition applies in the immediate area where a terrorist attack has occurred or when intelligence has been received that terrorist action against a specific location or person is likely. Normally, this Force Protection Conditions is declared as a localized condition.

Terrorist incidents over the years show a trend toward ever-increasing numbers of attacks and sophistication in methods. Terrorist methods include threats, bombing, kidnapping, hostage taking, hijacking, assassination, sabotage, arson, armed raids or attacks, and other measures to disrupt daily activities. Such actions occur rather routinely in some parts of the world, and almost anyone can become a potential victim. The attacks on the World Trade Center and Pentagon have shown that these attacks can occur within the United States as well.

On March 3, 1998, Islamic terrorist financier Osama bin Laden issued an anti-American "fatwa," or religious ruling, in which all Muslims were openly invited to undertake terrorist attacks against American civilians and allied interests worldwide. This "fatwa" does not differentiate between Americans dressed in military uniforms and civilians. We are all targets. The stated goal is to send the bodies of Americans home "in wooden boxes and coffins."

The threat of terrorism must be taken seriously by all personnel, especially those who travel regularly. It is now clear that NO U.S. outpost or installation can be considered a low security risk. All U.S. Government employees and supporting contractors are urged to intensify personal security practices while on travel outside the U.S.

DOE's List of "Sensitive" Countries

Algeria
Armenia
Azerbaijan
Belarus
China
Cuba
Georgia (Republic of)
India
Iran
Iraq
Israel
Kazakhstan
Kyrgyzstan
Libya
Moldova
North Korea
Pakistan
Russia
Sudan
Syria
Taiwan
Tajikistan
Turkmenistan
Ukraine
Uzbekistan